# Simply Green Giving

Collins
*An Imprint of HarperCollinsPublishers*

# Simply Green Giving

## Giving

Create Beautiful Gift Wrapping, Tags, and
Handmade Treasures from Everyday Materials

## Danny Seo

PHOTOGRAPHS BY JENNIFER LEVY

HarperCollins books may be purchased for educational, business, or sales promotional use. For information please write: Special Markets Department, HarperCollins Publishers, 10 East 53rd Street, New York, NY 10022.

FIRST EDITION

Designed by Lorie Pagnozzi
Photographs by Jennifer Levy

Library of Congress Cataloging-in-Publication Data

Seo, Danny.
    Simply green giving: create beautiful gift wrapping, tags, and handmade treasures from everyday materials / Danny Seo. — 1st ed.
            p. cm.
    ISBN 13: 978-0-06-112277-4
    ISBN 10: 0-06-112277-7
        1. Handicraft. 2. Recycling (Waste, etc.) 3. Environmentalism. I. Title.
TT160.S374 2006
745.—dc22

                                                              2006041246

06 07 08 09 10        ❖/QB      10 9 8 7 6 5 4 3 2 1

TO MY FAMILY,
FOR GIVING ME THE
SUPPORT IN MY EFFORTS
TO MAKE A DIFFERENCE
IN THE WORLD.

# Acknowledg

When creating a book on gift giving, it seems so appropriate to give thanks to all who worked so hard to bring this beautiful book together.

The wonderful team at Collins: Joe Tessitore, Mary Ellen O'Neill, Libby Jordan, George Bick, and Shelby Meizlik and Paul Olsewski. A special thanks to my wonderful editor, Matthew Benjamin.

To my dear friend who shot all the lovely photos in this book: Jennifer Levy.

My advisor through the literary world: Mary Evans. Much gratitude to my supportive team: Tom Carr, Jessica Fee, Claudine Gumbel, Matthew Lefferts, Emily Scofield, and everyone at CAA.

To all my partners and colleagues who share in my mission to prove green living can also be great, too: LIME TV and Radio, Kimpton Hotel & Restaurant Group, Rechargeable Battery Recycling Corporation, and *Country Home* magazine.

My charity partners at the Humane Society of the United States with a special thanks to Dr. John Grandy and Patricia Ragan. Many thanks to Stephane Jaspar for being a wonderful partner to the Humane Society's work.

And to all my friends who have given me the greatest gift of all: your friendship.

vii

# Contents

# Foreword

At the Environmental Media Association, we believe one way
to actually change the world is shopping!

Everywhere you look, from the news to magazines and even TV
sitcoms, there are references to living the green life as being good,
cool, and responsible. It is typical these days to see celebrities
pull up to red carpet events in their fuel-efficient hybrid cars.
And there is such an abundance of organic and natural skin care
products in the pages of fashion magazines that it seems the
chemically based, toxic-filled ones stick out like sore thumbs.
Even series television has characters carrying their groceries
in reusable cloth bags or tossing their cans and bottles into the
recycling bin! It may just be a set, but the message comes out loud
and clear: Green living just makes sense.

Today, Danny Seo is bringing green living to a whole new level with the publication of this gorgeously photographed lifestyle guide, *Simply Green Giving*. Green living is chic and fun.

Danny Seo has a flair and talent for mixing green living with a unique and stylish viewpoint on lifestyle in general. For example, he recycles a sheet of newspaper to wrap a bottle of organic wine. What's extraordinary isn't the fact that he uses newspaper—who hasn't wrapped a gift in the Sunday comics?—but *how* he wraps it. With just a few snips of the scissors, he shows us how to make the top of the bottle look like it's overflowing with hundreds of curls. The end result is a wrapped gift that is absolutely gorgeous. And it's also one of the greenest ways to wrap a gift.

Or how about his clever gift idea for the holidays: a mimosa kit. Just visit a thrift shop or antique store and pick up an inexpensive Champagne bucket. Fill with organic oranges, a citrus reamer, and a bottle of Champagne, and you've got the perfect, totally useful, and most easy-to-assemble present anyone would love to receive. Danny Seo tells us how some of the world's finest Champagnes have a history of being organic and how wineries are using modern technology today to avoid using harmful insecticides on their vines. This book is full of *a-ha!* moments like that.

As president of the Environmental Media Association, I work with the entertainment industry to bring environmental messages to the biggest audience possible, via films and television. These environmental messages are designed to both entertain and educate, and to inspire people to live a greener, leaner life. As I said before, we use celebrities to role-model green behavior . . . and shopping! Danny is someone who shares the same goal as we do: to actively work to protect the biodiversity of the planet, by inspiring people with fun and flair.

I really mean it when I say Danny's book *Simply Green Giving* is simply perfect. Read it, use it, and share it.

Debbie Levin
President,
Environmental
Media Association

# Introduction

Who hasn't faced this dilemma: figuring out how to wrap a present
when there isn't a stitch of gift wrap or ribbon in sight? Perhaps it's
an unwrapped bottle of wine you're bringing to a dinner party. Or a
lovely toy for your niece's birthday. And the granddaddy of them all:
the holiday season.

One Christmas, many years ago, I was at home with a stack of presents
on the kitchen table. After an exhausting day of shopping for the right
presents, I sat there staring at the pile of gifts and wondering who I had
forgotten. And it hit me: I failed to pick up gift wrap in my flurry of
shopping.

I went back to the store and waited in a long line to buy gift wrap.
Standing there, I looked at my arms full of shiny paper, all tightly
wound around cardboard tubes with shrink-wrapped plastic on top.
I had no idea how much wrapping paper I was actually getting. Once
home, I discovered those cardboard tubes are rather deceptive; there
seems there was more cardboard tube than actual paper! So, I went
back to the store to buy even more wrapping paper. After I was done
wrapping all the gifts, I had a mound of wrapping confetti: paper strewn
all over the floor along with crumpled cardboard tubes and plastic
wrap. I filled up an entire garbage bag full of this stuff and hauled
it out to the trash.

Despite the obvious ecological no-no here, I actually thought this small sacrifice for the planet might be worth it when my family saw how lovingly and beautifully I wrapped their presents. I waited for gushes and elation from my family as I handed the gifts out, but was only met with a flurry of hands shredding everything to little pieces. Boxes, ribbons, cards, and paper headed right into the trash. Then it dawned on me that I actually spent money on something that was invented to be ripped up and thrown away. Disgusted with the waste of resources and money, I vowed to never again buy gift wrap, cards, or ribbon.

To me, there is nothing less eco-friendly than wrapping a present. It's just more packaging on top of packaging. But as an environmentalist who is also a lifestyle expert, I find myself at a crossroads. On one hand, I didn't want to be wasteful by buying wrapping paper and ribbon, only to watch it be thrown away. On the other hand, I didn't want to hand an organic wool scarf to my friend, unwrapped, arms extended, and say, "Here, happy birthday. Enjoy."

Since that day, finding environmentally friendly alternatives to wrapping paper, ribbon, gift cards, and even the gift itself has been a slight obsession of mine. I've come up with ideas that have resulted in creations that are ecological *and*—this is a rather important point here—gorgeous. Sure, we've all heard of using newspaper to wrap gifts, but it looks boring and the ink gets all over your hands. There are better ways to do this. Instead, the ideas in this book are easy, affordable (if not free), and still have an element of unexpected surprise that elevates eco gift wrapping to an art form. I've also figured out clever ways to recycle ribbon, cards, and paper from presents people gave me. I even came up with a few last-minute gift ideas that don't look like an afterthought and are gifts people will actually love.

This book is packed with the best of the best. For example, you can make extraordinary, curly, shiny black bows by breaking open an old VHS tape and using the film inside. Just run strips of the tape along the edge of a sharp scissor and it curls right up. There is almost a limitless amount of this stuff inside of each VHS tape, so go nuts and make the most glamorous, over-the-top bows to adorn any gift. The best part is that it doesn't look recycled, but shiny, chic, and gorgeous.

Warmly,
**Danny Seo**

## A Special Note to the Reader

The *Simply Green* book series is printed on recycled content paper and produced without the addition of a dust jacket to save resources. All of the photography is done digitally, eliminating a significant amount of wasteful film and processing, all without sacrificing quality.

All of the actual props and materials used to produce the book—from the holiday cards to rolls of ribbon—were created using recycled, thrift-shop sourced, or truly organic fabrics and materials.

# Chapter 1

# CARDS AND TAGS

You may find this surprising, but even though e-mail invitations and online greeting cards are an ecological, tree-free choice, I am not a fan. I've always found something too convenient and impersonal about receiving something like a birthday greeting via e-mail. Something about the phrase, "Click here to view your greeting," turns me off.

I know there are many of you who agree with me that there is nothing more touching and personal than receiving a handwritten card, invitation, or even a gift tag from a loved one. Whenever I receive a beautiful note or card, I save them. Instead of photo albums to remind me of special events, handwritten notes do the trick for me.

Perhaps in a fast-paced, disposable world, making a gift tag by hand or handwriting a note on a card is one way to remind everyone to slow down.

This chapter is full of ideas to create unusual and ecological gift tags that you can use on all types of gifts, for all types of celebrations. If you've got a stash of cards tucked away in a drawer someplace, bring them out. I have a number of ideas how to display them, recycle them, and even transform them into something spectacularly decorative.

# BUSINESS-CARD GIFT TAG

**Two unwanted business cards**
**White craft glue**
**Hole punch**
**String**

These charming and useful gift tags are actually recycled from two unwanted business cards.

   Choose two cards that are identical in size, with at least one card completely blank on one side and the other card with an interesting graphic
element. Glue the printed fronts (the side that bears the business name,
address, phone, etc.) together using white craft glue. Allow to dry completely.
Fold the card in half and crease it with your fingernail to create a straight,
sharp line. Open the card and use the hold punch to place two holes directly
on the crease; run a string through the holes and tie a knot.

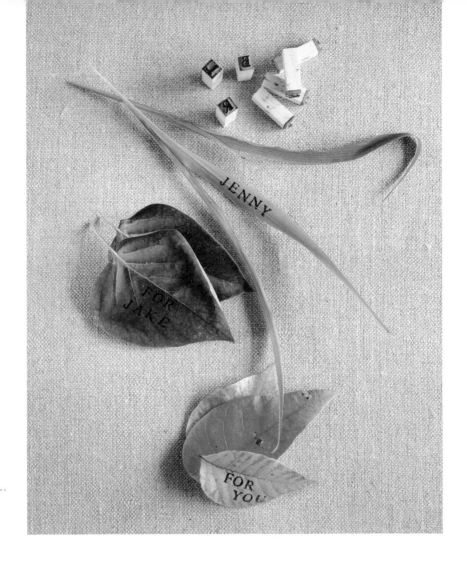

## LEAF AND GRASS LABELS

Mother Nature can be a limitless source of pretty gift tags, all free for the taking. Look for colorful leaves in the fall, large blades of grass in the summer, and even a stray feather left behind by a feathered friend. Use a set of alphabet stamps and a permanent ink pad to stamp out the gift recipient's name. After you tie a ribbon on the gift, tuck the natural tag into the bow.

# PHOTO-WATCH GIFT TAG

Old watches that are beyond repair can often be found at flea markets and thrift shops for very little money. For a special gift for a special friend, recycle them into a photo-watch gift tag.

Find the small notch on the back of the watch and use a putty knife to gently and carefully pry it off. Remove all the mechanicals on the inside, being careful not to scratch the crystal. Press a photo of the gift recipient against the glass and pop the watch back into place. If the gift is small enough, you can just wrap the watch around the gift; if it's a large present, remove the band and attach it with ribbon. Your friend can easily change the photo inside the watch and wear the watch. You can also use old pocket watches and lockets, too.

*Materials*

Microwaveable clear glycerin soap

Pyrex measuring cup

Soap dye

Square, rectangular, or round soap molds

Craft-store alphabet tiles

Bamboo skewer

Ribbon

Here's a gift tag that can become a useful gift itself. These tags are actually made from soap and are easy to make. This project works best when you are wrapping a multitude of gifts for a variety of people during the holiday season.

Be sure to use a clear glycerin soap; any other soap will be too opaque to clearly see what's embedded inside. Microwave the soap in a Pyrex measuring cup according to package instructions. Once melted, add a few drops of soap dye to your liking and stir. Fill the soap molds halfway and place in the freezer to harden.

Use alphabet tiles (such as Scrabble tiles) to write out the recipient's name, and place them place on top of the hardened soap. Pour additional melted soap on top and chill. Unmold the soap tags and use a bamboo skewer to make a hole; string with ribbon and attach to the present.

# Cards that grow

Millions of greeting cards are bought and given away every single year. In fact, the world's largest producer of cards, Hallmark, sells around 566 million cards annually. That's a lot of trees being cut down to make cards and matching envelopes.

One small company in Boulder, Colorado, is taking an interesting approach toward greeting cards by encouraging the recipient to literally bury the card after reading it: the company's cards actually grow.

Bloomin' Flower Cards was founded in 1995 as an alternative to traditional cards. Its cards are first handmade from 100-percent postconsumer recycled paper, meaning the paper used is the same stuff you and I put into recycling bins at work and at home.

The company embeds the cards with actual seeds—a mixture of both annual and perennial wildflower seeds—that will germinate when put in the ground. The card is biodegradable and will actually nourish the ground and act as a mulch to help the seeds sprout.

If you're crafty, you can make your own blooming cards at home. Just shred used paper (computer paper, newspaper, etc.) into small pieces, put in a blender, and add cold water. Blend it until it becomes a slushy pulp, and pour it over a fine mesh screen. (I use an old window screen.) Press the water out and let it dry. When it's still slightly moist, sprinkle with seeds and push them into the paper with your fingers. Place the card between layers of recycled paper towels and roll a rolling pin or wine bottle over it to squeeze the last remaining drops of water. Write a greeting on top and send.

If this sounds like too much work, you can always order from the Bloomin' Flower Card Company at www.bloomin.com.

## CARD LUMINAIRES

*Materials*

Two birthday or holiday cards

¹⁄₈-inch hole punch

Needle

Twine

Glass-enclosed candle or rechargeable light

Instead of keeping cards tucked away in a drawer, recycle them into candle luminaires and use them to decorate your home.

Start with two cards identical in size. Stack them on top of each other, both with the folded side to the left. With a hole punch, cut out holes along the open-side edge, approximately every ¹⁄₄ inch. Thread a needle with twine and sew the two cards together to create a box shape. Use a well-protected candle in a glass container or rechargeable light to illuminate the luminaire on the table; line up several along the length of table for dramatic effect.

Remember, never leave a burning candle unattended.

Please
Come

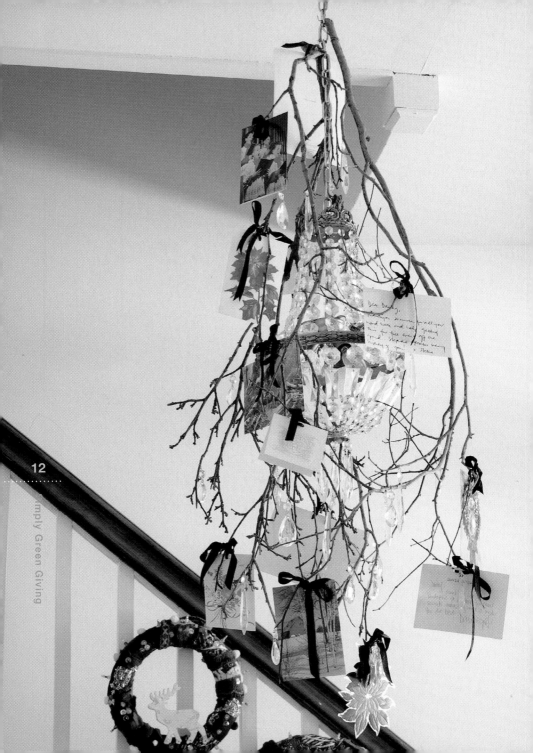

Simply Green Giving

# HOLIDAY-CARD BRANCH DISPLAY

Start a new tradition and hang cards and handwritten notes on branches in your home.

Gather branches from the yard; be sure to look for ones that are more gnarly with thin offshoots. Hang them from ceiling light fixtures (as pictured here) with 18-gauge wire, attached directly to the chain. Another idea is to display them in a tall vase (they will not need water) and place heavy rocks on the bottom of the vase to prevent it from tipping over.

Punch a hole in each card and attach the cards to the branches with thin ribbon or paper clips. Mix in photographs and mementos, such as vintage jewelry and ornaments, along with the cards.

TIP: While the most ecological way to say happy holidays is an online e-card, it isn't really the most thoughtful. I love to search thrift shops, Salvation Army stores, and flea markets all year long for vintage holiday cards at steeply discounted prices. You can find classic, glitter-encrusted cards from the 1950s to colorful, vintage-looking cards from the early 1980s. These weathered and antique-looking cards are an excellent environmentally friendly and memorable way to say "seasons greetings."

13

# Branching out

Call it practical or frugal, but I don't like to spend money on things I can get for free. In New York City, I always laugh when I walk by a flower stand selling a grouping of branches for a few dollars apiece. But New Yorkers buy them because it's scarce to find just lying around in the city nice, gnarly branches to add to your floral arrangements—that is, unless you're willing to go under the cover of darkness into Central Park, clippers in hand.

Branches are one of my staples that I use in the kitchen, in decorating, and in making crafts. I like to find young twigs and sharpen them in a pencil sharpener and use them to top a homemade caramel apple; the finished treats look more rustic and homey.

In the living room, gauzy organic cotton drapes hang from birch branches. Why pay tons of money for drapery hardware when you can get it for free in your own backyard?

And when I'm feeling particularly crafty, I'll get fat twigs and drill a hole down the middle and insert a pen refill to make twig pens. There's something charming about writing thank-you notes with a big, fat twig pen.

Branches can also be a cheap (translate: free) alternative to flowers. In the wintertime, you can snip branches from flowering trees like dogwoods. Bang the ends of the branches with a hammer (so they'll soak up water quickly) and place them in a very tall, very heavy (so it won't tip over) vase. Fill with warm water and wait a few days; in no time, leaves and flowers will sprout and create a gorgeous, tall flowering arrangement.

# CARD VILLAGES

**Three greeting cards**

**Scotch tape**

**Scissors**

**An old throw pillow (optional)**

Recycle a collection of cards into a charming holiday village. These paper homes are surprisingly simple and quick to make. This is a fun project you can do with the kids, too.

You'll need three cards that are identical in size. Tape two cards together to create a box shape. Cut out a door and windows; tape strips of paper inside the box to create window panes and add sheets of tissue paper, if desired. Cut the third card in half along the existing crease and tape each half to the sides of the box. Attach the two pieces together to create the finished roof.

Display the homes on a tabletop or mantel. To create a snowy effect, like the one pictured on the next page, rip open an unwanted throw pillow and use the polyester filling.

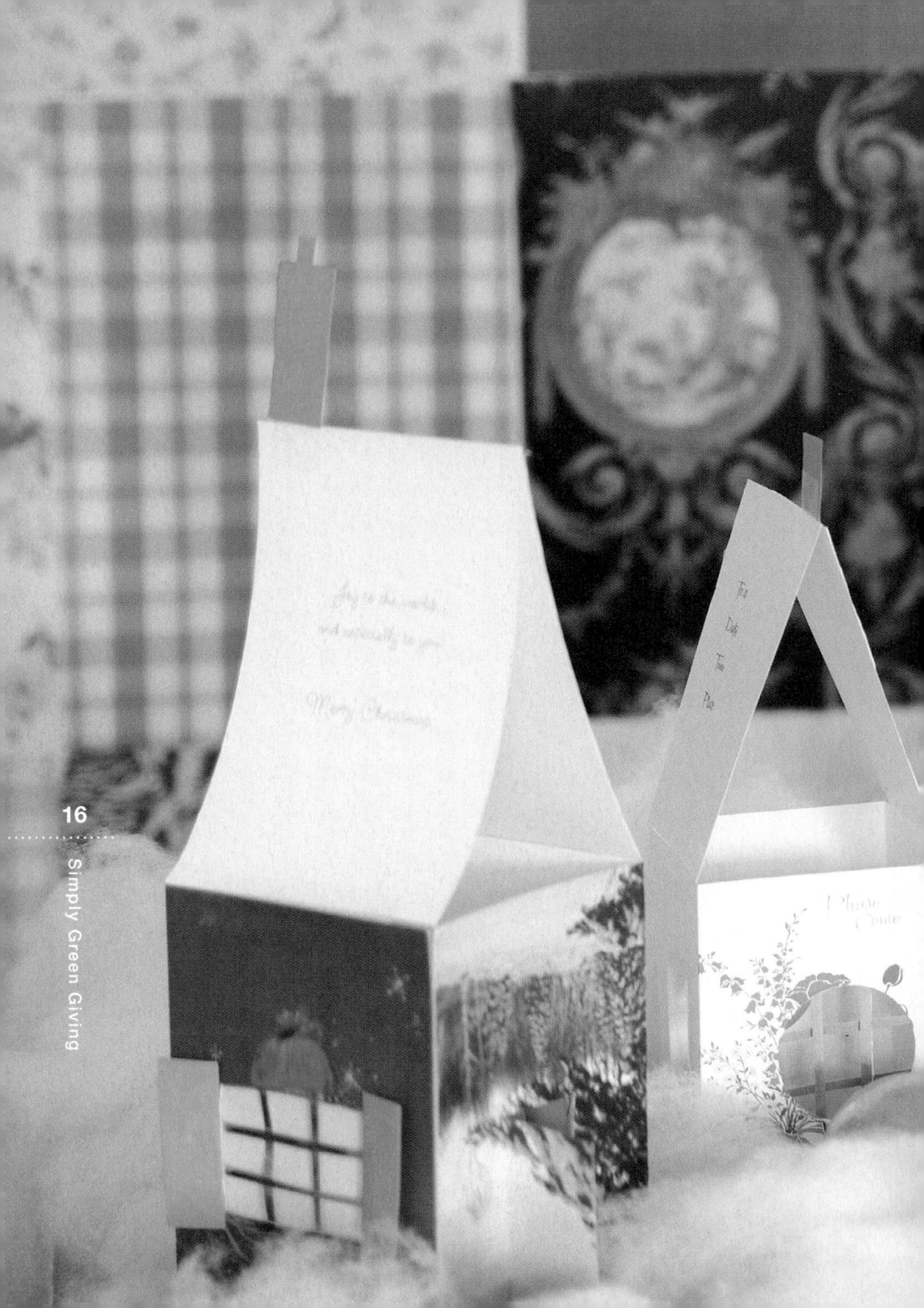

Chapter 2

# BOXES

There are just a handful of things in life that drive me bonkers: disposable cameras, Styrofoam cups, and flimsy gift boxes for sale in stores.

I've never had much success with the flat gift boxes with corners that "pop up" to make a three-dimensional box with its matching lid. I've always found them rather flimsy, and when you try to gift wrap them, the center of the boxes just caves back in. During the holiday season, stores give away millions of them every year—a regular environmental nightmare.

The idea of this chapter isn't to identify countless alternatives to gift boxes because, frankly, that would make for a rather boring chapter. There are plenty of free, eco-friendly alternatives all around us: used empty FedEx boxes, the cardboard box your inkjet printer came in, wine-store crates, and the countless boxes that held all those office supplies. It's simple: save these boxes and use them for gift giving.

Instead, this chapter is about thinking outside of the box, literally. Why not transform natural and everyday objects into surprising gift boxes that are so pretty they need little embellishment, and that the recipient will want to keep or reuse? Or make a gift box that can actually be a useful gift (see "Terra-Cotta Blooming Boxes")?

Now that I've gotten flimsy gift boxes off my chest, maybe I should rant about something else. That's right, I'm looking at you, Mr. I'm-talking-on-my-cell-phone-in-the-elevator-Man.

## CIGAR COOKIE BOXES

I am so opposed to cigarettes; my friends who do smoke know not to light up anywhere near my house. They find it quite ironic that one of my favorite shops to poke around in is a local cigar shop. You see, once the last cigar of a certain brand has been sold at these shops, all that's left is this gorgeous, handcrafted wood box. Many times, the owners will either give the boxes away or sell them dirt cheap. There's been more than one occasion where I've left the store with my arms full of cigar boxes, only to be spotted by a confused friend surely wondering, "I thought Danny didn't smoke?"

These are beautiful gift boxes, perfect for giving cookies or other freshly baked treats. Line the box with tissue paper, fill with the cookies, and add another layer of tissue on top. Snap the box closed and tie with ribbon. There's no need to wrap the boxes because the decorative markings and labels add a worldly embellishment all on their own.

TIP: Use these boxes to give gifts of scented candles, scarves, gloves, and jewelry. Whatever fits inside the box will work.

Simply Green Giving

# NATURAL BOX FILLERS

For Christmas one year, I sent all of my friends and business colleagues hand-poured soy candles in individual vintage glass molds. Since almost all of them needed to be shipped, I had to take extra care to package them properly, but was left with a dilemma in finding ecological alternatives to Styrofoam peanuts and plastic bubble wrap.

These box filler alternatives not only protect the contents in the box, but can also add a sense of drama to the overall gift. One friend, who received a candle protected by fresh pine needles, kept the box full of needles at her office desk because she loved the scent of the fresh pine.

Look to the great outdoors, supermarket aisle, and even your own recycling bins for filler alternatives.

- **From nature:** Use fresh pine needles cut directly from trees in your own yard or trim fragrant evergreen bushes; if it's the holiday season, prune your Christmas tree and use those branches.

- **From the yard:** Borrow fresh straw from the yard, or buy a bale of it from a local nursery if you plan on shipping multiple gifts. One bale is inexpensive, and leftover straw can be used as mulch in your own garden.

- **From the recycling bin:** Mix newspaper, office paper, and scent strips from magazines and put through a paper shredder. The scent strips will perfume the paper filler.

- **From the supermarket:** Instead of Styrofoam peanuts, use actual peanuts. Buy large, inexpensive bags of roasted peanuts (still in their shell) and surround the gift with them. Not only will the gift be protected, but the recipient can eat the peanuts.

- **From the trash:** When replacing bedroom or decorative pillows, save the filling. Rip the pillows open and use the fluffy contents to fill a box. When the box arrives at the destination, the cloud-like filler will make the gift presentation even more dramatic.

Any smooth container can become a firewood-inspired gift box. Make these wood-grained containers in a variety of sizes and have fun displaying them; stack them in a nonworking fireplace or carry them to a party in a firewood carrier.

Purchase wood-grained contact paper; this is available in the kitchen section of home improvement stores. Measure the container and cut a strip of contact paper the same height of the container. Wrap the paper all the way around the container and trim the excess paper. Remove the backing from the contact paper and adhere it. If it doesn't line up perfectly the first time, it's okay. The contact paper is repositionable and can be unpeeled easily and moved around.

Fill then with whatever needs a round container: a bottle of wine, an exquisite flavored vinegar, a stack of freshly baked cookies, jewelry, and even a lovely scarf.

# WOODLAND-TOPPED WOOD BOXES

*Materials*

**Craft-store unfinished wood boxes**

**Cordless drill with the smallest bit**

**Acorns**

**Eyelets**

There's a phrase I use all the time in my quest for new and interesting ideas: truth in materials. I love taking raw, unfinished objects, like a dusty pile of old marble tiles at the salvage yard, and turning them into useful items, like a stoveside trivet. I love letting their organic origins shine through with just enough embellishment.

One "truthful" item I love is unfinished wood boxes at the craft store. They come in a variety of sizes, are inexpensive, and I seem to find a new way to use them all the time.

Instead of painting or staining the boxes, I let the raw wood speak for itself and adorn them with box toppers like acorns. And it couldn't be simpler to do.

Remove the lid and drill a hole on the underside in the middle, using the smallest drill bit you have. Drill a hole in the middle of the acorn. Insert an eyelet on the inside of the box lid and screw it into acorn, twisting until it is firmly attached. You can also use twigs and pinecones as natural box toppers.

An unanticipated element of surprise can make a gift-giving experience even more special.

Recycle an unwanted large hardcover book into a surprise gift box. Vintage-looking books can be found at thrift shops if you don't have any books to spare—just make sure it isn't a priceless first edition. Use an X-acto knife to cut out a square hole inside the book. Tuck a ring, small gift, or even neatly folded up money inside the hole. Tie the box with ribbon.

TIP: Thrift shops are usually overrun with dictionaries and incomplete encyclopedia sets; pick up a few books and turn those into surprise gift boxes.

# Shopping at hardware stores with a different point of view

I'm amazed at how easy shopping has become. Today, you can get a fully cooked dinner *or* blinds for your windows "to go." Need new wall-to-wall carpeting? You can have it installed next day! Artificial Christmas trees are now sold pre-lit; just plug it into the wall to bring instant festive cheer indoors. You can even find bliss in a handy carrying case: spa-in-a-box.

Okay, I'm not a fan of convenience shopping. It seems to become more and more difficult to find shops that just sell raw, authentic materials to the general public. This is one of the reasons why I love hardware stores: not because I'm particularly into home repair or renovation, but because they offer a variety of interesting raw materials that lets my imagination run wild.

A few years ago, I was poking around the plumbing department and found a large metal pipe clamp for less than a dollar. I noticed that with a twist of the attached screw, the clamp got tighter and tighter. I figured you could fill the clamp with upright wine corks, and the clamp would keep them snug and in place. Voilà! Trivet. To this day, I'm not quite sure what a pipe clamp is really for, but I do know it makes one great trivet.

And that's my point: When shopping at a hardware store, don't look at things strictly for their intended purpose. Look at their properties instead. For example, while copper wire may be something an electrician uses, you'll notice how flexible it is, how it comes in different sizes, and how pretty it gets when an aged patina begins to show on it. What could you use the copper wire for? Maybe you could make a hand-bent wire hanger for your solar outdoor lights! Or maybe that garden bushel basket for sale in the landscaping department could become a handsome laundry basket at home. That giant roll of burlap? Cut off a sheet and wrap a bottle of wine with it. For just a few dollars, you can wrap dozens of bottles to your heart's delight.

# EVERGREEN-THATCHED BOXES

**Craft-store unfinished wood boxes**

**Cordless drill with an $\frac{1}{8}$-inch drill bit**

**18-gauge wire**

**Evergreen clippings, such as holly or boxwood**

Throughout Europe, older homes often feature thatched roofs that are made from densely packed vegetation like straw to keep the natural elements out. These wood boxes are inspired by these historical homes.

Start with a simple, unfinished wood box. Drill small holes along edge, about every $\frac{1}{2}$ inch across the top and bottom of the box lid. Insert strips of 18-gauge wire through the holes and secure by twisting the wire onto itself underneath the lid. Insert evergreen clippings underneath the wire and thatch them into place. The evergreens should remain fresh and intact for several weeks, depending on variety.

TIP: For a less "holiday" appearance for your thatched box, consider swapping in old silk flowers instead. They'll give the box a springlike look and last forever.

## TERRA-COTTA BLOOMING BOXES

This is a great gift for friends who like to garden: a terra-cotta box filled with spring bulbs.

Fill a terra-cotta pot with enough flowering bulbs or seeds for two pots and a small bag of potting soil. Flip a matching terra-cotta pot on top, so the two edges of the pots meet. Secure them in place by tying a piece of ribbon around them.

## BAMBOO-STEAMER CARRYING TRAYS

The problem when traveling with freshly baked treats is that decorative trays do a poor job at protecting the goodies from breakage, and food storage containers do a poor job at being decorative. The solution is a Chinese bamboo steamer. Not only is it attractive and effective at protecting food, it can also be a gift.

Most bamboo steamers can be found at good kitchen supply stores or at an Asian market. They come in a variety of sizes and tiers; larger ones can accommodate pies and tarts and smaller ones can be used to carry cookies, hors d'oeuvres, and other smaller treats. Fill each tier with different treats and stack the steamer trays on top of each other. Wrap a decorative ribbon around the whole thing to keep it together.

# Scavenging at the office

Your place of business can be a treasure trove of supplies and tools to help you create gorgeously wrapped Simply Green gifts. Whether it's after hours or when the boss is away, take a peek around for unwanted materials and supplies that can make your gift-giving process more ecological and economical.

Some of the easiest things to find at offices are glass vases. There always seems to be a collection of mismatched vases tucked away under a sink in the commissary or shoved into an office supply closet. Pull them out and customize them into personalized flower vases (see Personalized Flower Vases in Chapter Four).

Use the paper shredder to make gift filler. Tear out pages in an unwanted magazine and run it through the shredder; add a few perfume advertisements into the mix to scent the shredded paper. Use this to keep delicate gift items protected or as filler in a gift basket.

And speaking of gift baskets, be on the lookout for those, too. How many times have you seen a collection of cheap wicker baskets just sitting atop filing cabinets or strewn about on the floor? Sure, at one point they held delicious, ripe fruit, but now they are just collecting dust. You can make them pretty by painting them black, using a glossy paint. Fill the stark, black basket full of vibrant, organic oranges and you've got a modern gift anyone would love.

Finally, look for unwanted boxes to recycle into gift boxes. Those sturdy cardboard boxes that hold reams of paper are an excellent choice for bulky presents. Used FedEx and UPS boxes can hold a thick sweater (and can be recycled and reused to ship the gift, too!).

# What to do with all those CDs?

The Digital Age is upon us, and it seems more and more things are becoming obsolete in our lives. First, VHS tapes were replaced by DVDs (which will soon be replaced altogether with video-on-demand). Now digital music is slowly turning compact discs into a thing of the past. As we amass unwanted CDs (and collect them from unsolicited mailings to join various online service providers!), the question remains: What to do with all these shiny discs?

I have heard many people suggest using them as coasters on a table. I can't tell you how much I dislike this idea. First of all, how many coasters do you really need? And secondly, why would you want to use a badly scratched, ugly disc on your nice table to begin with?

The coolest thing I have figured out to do with recycled CDs is to turn them into a dumbbell. I used a threaded rod from the hardware store about 18" in length (again, not sure what the rod is actually used for in the real world, but it worked perfectly for this project). I threaded about 25 CDs on each side of the rod and kept them in place by using a washer and a bolt to tighten it. When finished, the whole thing weighed about five pounds. I found it to be the perfect weight to use when doing crunches at home. To my surprise, the edges of the CDs are quite dull, so the whole thing could safely be placed right onto my stomach as I attempted to find the missing steel in my abs.

Another idea is to shred them. Many paper shredders today have a separate slot for CDs and credit cards for safe slicing and dicing. Use the shredded, silvery mess as gift filler in a small gift box.

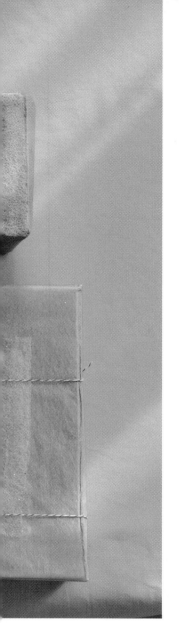

## DRYER-SHEET FROSTED BOXES

*Materials*

**Brown-paper grocery store bags**

**Evergreen clippings**

**Used dryer sheets**

**Stitch Witchery fabric-binding tape**

**Iron**

**String or ribbon**

Here's a clever way to recycle used dryer sheets after they've taken their tumble in the dryer.

Cut open a paper grocery-store bag and use the unprinted side to wrap a present. Place a selection of flat evergreen clippings on top and cover with the dryer sheet. You must use a used dryer sheet because a fresh one will still have embedded fragrance on the sheet that may leave an oily stain on the package. Cut Stitch Witchery tape (a web-like tape that bonds two fabrics together) to the dimensions of the dryer sheet and place the strips underneath, as close to the edge of the dryer sheet as possible. With an iron on a low-to-medium setting (with no steam), iron the dryer sheet and Stitch Witchery on top of the gift, binding it all to the wrapped gift for a few seconds on each side. Finish by tying string or ribbon around the gift.

# Simply green and beautiful bamboo

In my book, *Conscious Style Home*, I showed how I renovated my parents' Pennsylvania home into a living, breathing eco-friendly model home. One of the first things I did was remove the crumbling vinyl tile and replace it with gorgeous bamboo flooring.

When the book was published, bamboo flooring was still considered an exotic material. It was also hard to source, and I had to go all the way to California to find a supplier willing to sell it to me.

Today is a whole different story. Bamboo flooring is almost as common as hardwood flooring. And it's easy to see why: it's beautiful, sustainable, and surprisingly affordable.

Bamboo is a *Simply Green* choice because even though it has the look and appearance of wood, it isn't wood; it's a fast-growing grass with very woody stems. Native to tropical, subtropical, and temperate regions, bamboo grows quickly, as much as one foot *per day*. Even though large, beautiful bamboo plants may be harvested to produce flooring, these plants can regenerate overnight.

Now that we're accustomed to bamboo flooring, I want you to look for the many other bamboo products in the marketplace. Perhaps you've had bamboo shoots in a delicious Asian dish, savoring each bite with bamboo chopsticks, while sitting on gorgeously lacquered bamboo chairs. There are even soft-as-silk textiles spun from bamboo that are being used by top designers in their collections.

Even though I advocate sifting through thrift shops and junk stores for vintage boxes, notions, and gift items, there are times when buying something new is just easier and more time efficient. In those cases, you can feel good in buying anything bamboo because it is a renewable resource that is durable and gorgeous to look at. Look for bamboo serving trays, coasters, boxes, desk organizing accessories, floor and table mats, and much more. Use these bamboo items as the base for your present or just tie them all up with a pretty ribbon. You simply cannot go wrong with bamboo.

# TWIN TRAYS AS A CARRYING CASE

Carrying homemade appetizers on a decorative tray to a special event, such as a housewarming or a potluck, can be a challenge. The only way to keep the appetizers protected is to either store them in ugly plastic storage containers (and then transfer them to platters at the event) or wrap layers of plastic cling wrap to the tray. Here's an ecological and prettier alternative.

You'll need two identical platters or trays to make an instant carrying case. Densely fill one tray with your appetizers to the point where they won't shift when carried. Invert the other tray on top to act as a lid and tie the whole thing together with ribbon. At the party, untie the ribbon and place half the appetizers on the other tray.

TIP: If you are bringing treats to a housewarming party, consider giving the host or hostess the two trays as a present.

Chapter 3

# GIFT WRAP
## AND BOWS

Like other kids growing up, I had a role model who was on television. But unlike other kids, I didn't really want to *be* my role model, Mac-Gyver, nor did I really follow the plotlines carefully on his television show. Instead, I think I was obsessed with the idea of him—or to be more precise—one of his personality traits.

MacGyver was the television spy, played by actor Richard Dean Anderson, who solved adventurous crimes all over the world, and did it all without the use of a gun. Instead, he ingeniously would get out of jams and terrifying situations by being resourceful and using what he had on or around him. Stuck in a Turkish cell? He would use a shard of glass, the rays from the hot sun, and a piece of lint to somehow create a detonating device.

MacGyver is perhaps one of the reasons why, today, I am obsessed with finding new uses for old things.

I couldn't help but remember my childhood obsession with MacGyver as I worked on this chapter. Stuck in my home one wintery afternoon, I avoided cabin fever by going through my pantry, basement, and desk drawers and seeing if any inspiration would strike me. Could the inside of a potato-chip bag be used as gift wrap? What could I do with electrical tape? Many of my favorite ideas came from that creativity-fueled afternoon.

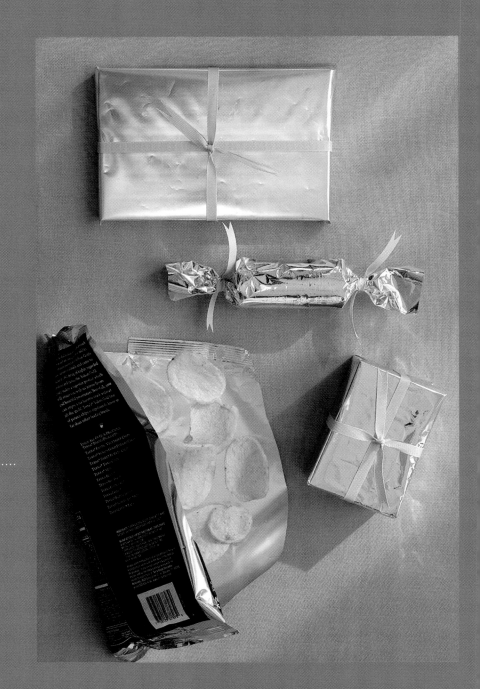

## POTATO-CHIP-BAG WRAP

These shiny wrapped gifts look so chic and ultra-mod. But despite their fashionable appearance, they are actually wrapped with just a bag from potato chips.

Save snack-food bags that have a silvery, shiny lining. Carefully snip the bags open along one edge to flatten them and wash them thoroughly with warm, sudsy water. (I do this whenever I'm washing the dishes to save time.) Once dry, use it as gift wrap!

TIP: If you want to wrap larger gifts, tape several flattened bags together until you achieve the desired size piece.

47

# BURBERRY-INSPIRED GIFT WRAP

**Brown-paper grocery-store bags**

**Scissors**

**Electrical tape in different colors (e.g., red, black, and white)**

The Burberry plaid pattern is a fashion icon almost as recognizable as the American flag's patriotic hues of red, white, and blue. This simple gift-wrapping idea pays homage to the House of Burberry. And a little bit of artist Piet Mondrian.

Open a paper grocery-store bag with a pair of scissors to make it a flat piece of paper. Don't worry about creases or wrinkles; you can stretch them out if you wrap the gift tightly enough. Wrap the gift with the paper, making sure the unprinted side shows on the outside of the finished wrapped package. Use electrical tape (found at any home improvement store) and adhere strips of red, black, and white tape around the package in a random pattern using different colors. For straight lines, run the tape around the box when it's still on the roll and then snip off the excess. Doing this will help you control the neatness of the stripes.

**TIP:** If you have leftover electrical tape, use it to dress up a small tabletop, mirror, or wood stool.

48

## SCARF-WRAPPED WINE BOTTLES

**Scarf**

**Large safety pin**

I love gift-wrapping ideas that actually become presents. This is a great idea when giving a gift of wine or spirits during the winter months. Thinner fabric scarves work best for this type of gift wrap.

Start at the bottom of the wine bottle with one end of the scarf and wrap it around and around; the tighter you wrap it, the more secure the scarf will be. When you get to the top of the bottle, pin the end of the scarf onto itself as tightly as possible. Pull some of the excess fabric through the top hole to make it "flower" a little bit. Try a sequin scarf when wrapping something festive like champagne.

51

# NEWSPAPER-WRAPPED FESTIVE BOTTLES

*Materials*

**Newspaper**

**Scotch tape**

**Ribbon or string**

**Scissors**

I know, I've gone on the record against using newspaper to wrap gifts. But for a quick and gorgeous way to wrap a bottle of wine, this technique seems to shine when using newspapers. The best part is you also need only scissors and tape to make this work.

Begin with two layers of newspaper and wrap them around the bottle, leaving about 5 inches of excess newspaper above the top of the bottle. Use a piece of tape to keep the newspaper snug around the bottle. Tie a ribbon or string around the neck of the bottle. With a pair of scissors, cut strips down from the top of the paper to the top of the bottle. Run each newspaper strip along the sharp edge of the scissors until it curls.

TIP: If you're bringing a bottle of wine to a housewarming, use the real estate pages from the newspaper.

## OFFICE COPY-ROOM RECYCLING

Inspiration and ideas can come from anywhere, and in this case, it comes from the recycling bins at the office or local photocopy shop.

Photocopies of anything and everything seem to always end up in the recycling or trash bin. Look for oversized sheets of color-copy rejects (photographs, charts, graphs, etc.) and use them to wrap presents. When the image is wrapped, folded, and cut to fit a box, it takes on an unusual and indistinguishable look. Is that a catalog page? Is that a woman's face smiling at me?

Also, look for oversize calendar pages or those giant flip-chart pads used in conference rooms. The more scribbled notes, ideas, and bullet points on these giant sheets, the more Stephen Sprouse–graffiti-inspired the gift wrap looks.

55

One of my favorite shops is a Goodwill outlet store in Shillington, Pennsylvania. Here you won't find racks of used things, but big white bins full of unwanted castoffs that couldn't be sold at other Goodwill shops. In a way, it's the last chance for the items to be rescued before being dumped. And the prices can't be beat: Everything is sold by weight, just pennies a pound.

Clothes, books, vases, cooking supplies—you name it—commingle with each other. I love standing there digging through the piles and discovering glorious treasures: antique Le Creuset cookery (fifty cents), a vintage tie from Abercrombie & Fitch (back when it was a hunting goods company [ten cents]), and a gorgeous faux-bois wood-grained Christmas-tree stand (twenty-five cents).

On one visit, I saw a huge pile of well-worn work-shirts: soft plaid flannel, thick cotton denim, and other types of cotton shirts. That's when the idea of using them as gift wrap got stuck in my head.

Using shirts to wrap gifts couldn't be simpler. Cut off the sleeves, wrap them around a bottle, and use ribbon to keep them snug and in place. Cut out the back part of the shirt as a flat piece of gift wrap; pull it around the gift and tie a piece a ribbon on top. XXL-size shirts mean extra fabric. Try using pieces that have elements of the shirt such as buttons, sleeves, and collars for added effect. For an additional decorative touch, use fabric pinking shears to create a zigzag edge.

I tend to use only plaid shirts, but if you find something else that strikes your interest, go for it!

# Tips on shopping at thrift shops

If you're like me, you don't define your style by what the label says on your clothes or by how much you paid for a vase to decorate your home. Instead, you seek out things that are stylish, unconventional, and just outright beautiful, no matter where you found them. Throughout my house and wardrobe, you'll find a mix of new and old, upscale and vintage, and splurges and steals that all somehow meld together to showcase a sense of style that is all my own.

My local Goodwill, Salvation Army, and junk stores continue to serve as endless inspiration for new crafty ideas, such as recycling work shirts into fabric gift wrap. I also find amazing pieces for my home and wardrobe that are usually for sale for next to nothing but are priceless in my book.

Over the years, I've learned a few tips to find those priceless treasures in these shops. After all, *Simply Green Giving* should also be about giving something to yourself. With these tips, you'll find something incredible at your local thrift shop, too.

· **Visit out-of-the-way locations.** Secondhand shops in major metropolitan areas are often "picked over." In fact, there are professional shoppers called pickers whose sole job is to go through these shops and buy all the good vintage clothing and accessories, all to be resold in upscale shops around the country. Perhaps on your next trip to visit a distant relative or on your next business trip you should take some time to visit local charity shops and thrift shops to seek out hidden treasures. In Pennsylvania, I'll sometimes drive an hour to a small building that serves as a Goodwill shop to the Amish; I'll find charming things the Amish donated that they consider trash: antique canning jars, vintage ribbons and notions, and fabrics. I guess one Amish person's trash is my treasure!

· **Shop for the basics.** You are not always going to find a first edition of *Gone with the Wind* in the five-cents book bin each time. Think basics the next time you feel crafty. Reglazing a plate? Pick up basic ceramic plates for next to nothing. Making the silk-flower gift toppers described in this book? I bet at the local Salvation Army you'll find a big plastic bag of ugly silk flowers you can transform into a thing of beauty.

· **Dig deep.** When you shop in a fancy store, everything for sale is usually set out so simply and beautifully that your eyes can do the shopping. In a thrift shop, that's not the case—you have to dig deep. Go through stacks of plates, one plate at a time. Pick up piles of books and see what may be lurking underneath. Throw your body deep into a bin of fabrics and find out if that glimmer way down deep is a sterling-silver bowl.

· **Become a friend.** Ask the people running the shop when new items come in or when they usually bring out fresh stock from the back room. If it's always 9:00 A.M. everyday, be at the shop at 9:05 A.M.

# RESOURCEFUL WRAPPING

Originally, this idea was never supposed to be in this book. After all, how many people have leftover spools of "Admit One" tickets lying around the house?

I think this idea is a good example of resourcefulness. When I threw a charity event a few years ago, I ended up with thousands of these colorful tickets and stashed them away. Eventually I pulled them out and have been using them to wrap small gifts.

The idea here is we all amass unusual things that we'll never know what we're going to do with that end up in our closets, junk drawers, attics, and garages. There might be the extra yards of lace fabric from a wedding or stacks of construction paper your kids didn't like. Pull 'em out, cut 'em up, and get wrapping.

TIP: Heading to the fairground with the kids? Not sure what to do with that stack of skee-ball prize tickets? Save 'em and try this ticket-wrapped project.

## BANDANNA-WRAPPED GIFTS

I love bandannas because they are inexpensive and have a multitude of uses. They can be handy napkins at the dinner table, colorful sachets in the dresser drawers, and Western-inspired pillows for the living room.

Simple, colorful bandannas can also become fancy fabric gift wrap all with a twist of the wrist and a piece of string. Center the gift in the middle of the bandanna and bring up the sides of the fabric until it's taut around the gift. Twist the fabric so it creates pretty folds, and tie it all together with a piece of string. Pull the fabric up through the string if the bandana is too loose.

# SCENTED BOWS

**Perfume-advertisement scent strips**

**Stapler**

**Scissors**

**Double-stick tape**

I love free things, and those scented perfume strips found in fashion magazines are absolutely fantastic in my opinion. It's become a slight obsession of mine to find new and interesting ways to recycle these scent strips. In *Simply Green Parties,* I used them to make a bouquet of paper flowers. Here's another idea: scented paper—bow gift toppers.

Carefully remove the scent strips from a magazine as neatly as possible. Open the scent strip and cut ½-inch strips across the sheet, starting from the scented side and stopping about an inch from the end.

Fold the paper onto itself like a fan, taking extra care to make sure the cut strips remain intact and neatly stacked against each other. When you reach the end, staple the uncut section so it stays together. With a pair of sharp scissors, curl each strip against the blade; the harder and quicker you run the strip against the blade, the curlier it will get.

When finished, use double-stick tape to attach the scented bow to the package.

TIP: After the bow's been taken off the package, put it on a warm radiator for about an hour; the perfume will permeate the air.

# PATCHWORK-RIBBON REMNANTS

**Ribbon remnants**

**Stitch Witchery fabric-binding tape**

**Iron**

This is one of those ideas that when I thought of it, I immediately questioned, "Now why haven't I thought of this sooner?"

When wrapping presents with new ribbon, you often end up with remnants of ribbon either at the end of the roll or when trimming excess ribbon off a present. Or when you receive a gift, you save bits and pieces, hoping to use them in the future one way or another. Here's an inventive way to recycle small bits of ribbon into a charming patchwork ribbon that can be made to dress up even the largest of gifts.

Sort ribbon remnants by width, such as ½- and 1-inch piles. Cut the Stitch Witchery tape into ¼-inch slivers that are also equal to the width of the ribbon. Place four Stitch Witchery slivers at the end of one piece of ribbon and place another ribbon on top. Using an iron on a low setting, place the iron on top and slowly press it for a few seconds until the Stitch Witchery melts and binds the two ribbons together. Repeat the process with the other remnants.

# RIBBON MEMORY BALLS

**Ribbon remnants**

**Pins**

**Styrofoam balls**

**Permanent fine-tip marker**

For special occasions like a child's birthday, baby shower, or wedding, create these ribbon memory balls. They look good all year round, so feel free to display them in a pretty bowl or on a table, just like the ones pictured here.

Collect ribbons from a special event and cut them into 2-inch strips. Randomly pin the ribbon strips all over a Styrofoam ball (available at any craft store); if you don't want to use foam, you can make smaller memory balls using old tennis balls. Be sure to cover the entire surface. Using a permanent fine-tip marker, write the details of the special event on one strip of ribbon somewhere on the ball, such as "Christmas 2006."

69

## UNUSUAL RIBBON

Sure, being green helps save the planet, but it also teaches you valuable skills in resourcefulness and creativity. If you want to add a touch of whimsy to a plainly wrapped gift, look no further than around your own home. People love imaginatively wrapped gifts, and this sure is one they'll find memorable.

Use a pair of spare shoelaces, burnt-out Christmas lights, colorful measuring tape, and even an unused belt to embellish a gift. The ideas are limitless. Look through your closets, the garage, and basement for things that can dress up any present into something fun and unexpected.

# Keeping jewelry
# sparkling clean

A visit to almost any flea market, thrift shop, or junk store will usually result in boxes or drawers jam-packed with a variety of vintage jewelry. While the more expensive diamond and precious stone pieces get passed down generation-to-generation or sold in pricey antique shops, you can usually find all types of older costume charms, pins, rings, earrings, and bracelets for next to nothing. Vintage also means *age*, but that's no reason to pass on jewelry simply because of dirt or tarnish. Try these Simply Green ways to revive vintage jewelry.

- **Silver-plated jewelry.** This tip is like magic: You can magnetize the tarnish away. Simply line the bottom of a bowl with a sheet of aluminum foil and fill the bowl with warm water. Add a generous amount of salt—about 4 tablespoons—and a squirt of liquid dish soap. Place the tarnished jewelry on top, and voila! You'll see the tarnish begin to disappear—a natural chemical reaction that actually magnetizes the tarnish right off. No buffing or rubbing needed. Wipe clean and dry with a terry towel. This also works wonders on tarnished flatware and silver-plated home accessories.

- **Rhinestones.** If that cubic zirconia gemstone ring is beginning to look more faux than fierce, give it a good cleaning. Fill a bowl with warm water and add liquid dish soap. Let the jewelry soak for a bit and use an old toothbrush (the older and more worn, the better; newer brushes will be a bit too abrasive) to loosen dust and dirt away. If you need a bit more help getting them clean, add a tiny bit of ammonia to the water and soak and brush again.

- Watches. Over time, wristwatches with metal bands can collect dead skin, dust, and dirt in between the links, hinges, and mechanical parts. If you have a waterproof watch, a quick way to keep it clean is to soak it in the bathroom sink with sudsy water, rinse clean, and then use a Q-tip to pick up dirt in between each link. If you have an espresso maker with a steam nozzle, you can use that to steam away the dirt, too. Just be sure to use something to protect your hands from the hot steam, like miniature tongs or extra-strong tweezers.

- Copper. Gourmet cooks have used salt and lemon juice to keep their copper pots gleaming; the citric acid from the lemon helps neutralize the tarnish away, and the salt acts as an abrasive. You can try the same technique when cleaning large copper pieces like a chunky bracelet. Just cut a lemon in half and squeeze lemon juice all over the copper piece. Sprinkle with salt (the juice will help the salt adhere) and use the lemon wedge to rub the salt all over the piece. Rinse clean under warm water in the sink. For smaller copper pieces, try the magnetizing trick used on silver-plated pieces; you'll get similar results.

# VHS TAPE RIBBON

**Old VHS tapes**
**Screwdriver**
**Scissors**

This is an idea that I've used so many times that I've actually run out of tapes at home and have been buying discarded VHS tapes at my local Goodwill. I can only imagine what the checkout clerk must've been thinking as I bought dusty copies of *Buns of Steel* and *Learn Your ABCs*!

VHS tapes are quickly becoming obsolete in a digital world. Inside these cassettes is an endless amount of shiny tape that can be recycled into chic ribbon for any gift. And it couldn't be easier to do.

Use a screwdriver to unhinge the small screws holding the tape together. Remove the spools inside the tape that hold the black tape and use it just like ribbon. Snugly tie the black tape into place and leave extra-long strands. Using a pair of sharp scissors, run the tape along the blade to create curly bows.

TIP: The tape from old cassettes and eight-track tapes can also be used as ribbon.

75

# SILK-FLOWER GIFT TOPPERS

**Thrift-shop silk flowers**

**Florist tape**

**Scissors**

Whenever I visit my local thrift shops, there is always an abundance of tacky silk flower arrangements for sale, sometimes even marked with a price tag reading "free." I'm not a fan of artificial flowers for home décor, but they can be a colorful and lovely addition to wrapped gifts. Pull silk flowers out of the attic, or pick them up for next to nothing at your local thrift shop, and make these blooming silk-flower gift toppers.

Begin by removing the plastic leaves off each stem; they add bulk and only make the silk flowers look less real. Group flowers together by color and wrap florist tape around the stems, starting as close to the petals as possible and working your way down. If the stems are too long, use a pair of sharp scissors (or gardening shears) and snip the stems. Place the bouquet on top of a gift and tie into place with ribbon.

TIP: There's no need to be horticulturally correct when making silk-flower gift toppers; feel free to mix and match flowers by colors, instead of type.

77

CHAPTER THREE: Gift Wrap and Bows

# Books-a-million

Filling a room with books is one of the easiest ways to bring a sense of coziness to the space. Other than filling your bookshelves, you can also recycle books into new and charming decorative accessories.

- **Wallpaper the walls.** One of my celebrity clients loves to collect older children's books that she finds in thrift shops and library used-book sales. She'll carefully cut out illustrated pages and decoupage them onto the walls as if they are small squares of wallpaper. The end result is surprisingly charming: An outdoor bunkhouse dedicated to reading is totally covered in vintage pages from old encyclopedias. You can use the same idea for your kid's room by using pages from charming, illustrated children's books.

- **Make a book clock.** Recycle a handsome hardcover book into something totally utilitarian. Most craft stores sell make-your-own clock kits—complete with all the mechanisms you need to turn almost anything into a functioning clock. All you have to do is follow the kit's instructions: Drill a hole in the middle of your book and cut out a square big enough inside to fit the battery-powered clock box. Insert battery, close the book, and it becomes a real, working clock. Try transforming an old cookbook and hang it in the kitchen.

- **Make a bookshelf.** You can transform a boring wall shelf with some old hardcover books. Simply find hardcover books large enough to conceal the top, side, and bottom of the shelf. Rip out enough pages inside the book so you can "wrap" the book around the shelf; use wood glue to attach the book to the shelf. Keep adding books until the whole shelf is covered. When you're done, it'll look like a shelf made entirely out of books.

Chapter 4

# HANDMADE
## GIVING

We've all heard the phrase, "It's the thought that counts." Frankly, I'm not sure who came up with that saying because if I were to choose between a box of home-baked cookies and the hybrid car of my dreams, I can honestly say I would be more ecstatic about the car.

Extravagance aside, I do believe thoughtful gifts can be touching when you take the time to *think* about the recipient and what gift would really cause true adoration and joy.

That's why I wanted to share some simple, handmade ideas so you can create and give gifts that will not only delight your friends and family, but are thoughtful for both the recipient and the planet.

The idea of this chapter isn't about teaching you labor-intensive crafting skills, so don't expect step-by-step instructions on glazing a pot or crocheting a rug. Instead, these are simple gift ideas that can be made with a quick trip to the supermarket, antique store, or flea market. I love finding older, vintage items—not necessarily antiques (translation: not pricey)—but quirky things that no chain store will have in stock. Mix them with the best organic fruits, a good bottle of biodynamic wine, or a selection of all-natural bath products and you can't go wrong.

*Materials*

**Cardboard globe**

**Serrated knife (optional)**

**Shredded filler (newspaper or raffia)**

**Selection of organic fruits**

**Cellophane**

**Ribbon**

If you're like me, your childhood bedroom had one of those cardboard globes that spun around on a metal stand and identified the former Soviet Union as USSR. It's time to pull it out of the attic or basement and transform it into a global treat that any food lover will adore. And here's the best part: each globe will make two complete gifts for you to give.

Find the equator on the globe and peel off the tape that's holding the two halves of the globe together. Once the tape is removed, you should be able to twist the halves apart, or you can use a serrated knife to do so. From the inside of the globe, unscrew the mechanisms that hold it to the metal stand.

Fill each half of the globe with shredded filler and place a selection of unblemished, good-quality organic fruits. In this bowl, I used pomegranates, blood oranges, mangoes, grapefruit, and pears. Wrap each globe with a big sheet of clear cellophane and tie with ribbon.

P.S. Did you know cellophane is good for the environment? It's made from tree pulp, also known as cellulose, which makes it biodegradable. Sheets of cellophane can be placed directly into the compost bin and should decompose within thirty days.

## FOR A SWEET SURPRISE: VINTAGE JEWELRY TREATS

Give an assortment of vintage jewelry by presenting it in an empty chocolate or candy box. Save the plastic compartment and place individual pieces—charms, pins, rings, earrings—in each slot. Wrap some pieces up in colorful tissue paper and tie with string; they'll be gifts within the gift.

Shop estate sales, flea markets, and antique stores to find an assortment of vintage pieces.

## FOR A SURPRISE:
## 3-D PORTRAIT "GIFT" PAINTING

I love a good bargain. Check out yard sales and flea markets for inexpensive portraits and recycle them from two-dimensional works of art into three-dimensional canvases for gift giving.

Pin vintage earrings, necklaces, pins, and rings (if a hand is visible in the painting) directly onto the painting. Be creative: add sparkly jewels to a landscape or transform a print of dogs playing poker into dogs giving gifts.

TIP: If you don't want to poke holes though the paining, try double-stick tape or a florist adhesive to place jewelry directly onto the painting.

## FOR THE SWEET TOOTH:
## COOKIES-AND-MILK CRATE

As far as handmade gifts go, this one is a real tasty one, full of sweet treats and wholesome milk to wash it all down.

Save wooden crates when you buy tangerines or ask your local farmers' market for the wooden boxes that their produce comes in. Fill the box with an assortment of your favorite cookies and add a bottle or two of organic regular and chocolate milk. Try to find milk in charming glass bottles at your local farmers' market. If it's the holidays, add a candy cane or two for color and festive cheer.

# A gift so good you can eat it

One of the most practical and ecological gifts you can give is the gift of food. You don't have to worry about sizes and the only good taste you need is literally just that: give the tastiest, freshest, and most decadent things you can find.

Gifts of food can also be thoughtful presents. Many people have adopted specific dietary choices into their lives, and when you give a gift that reflects that, it shows you care. Some thoughtful edible gifts ideas include:

- **For the vegan:** Shop health-food stores and online vegan shops, such as www.veganessentials.com, for exotic and delicious nondairy chocolate truffles, gelatin-free marshmallows, and egg- and dairy-free cookies, cakes, and other sweet treats. Since most vegans miss bakery treats, pack them all up in a pink bakery box and tie with string so your animal-loving friends can get that nostalgic feeling they had during their pre-vegan days.

- **For the low carber:** For those who love meat, take the effort to source high-quality, sustainable meats from farmers who raise "heritage" foods. Heritage Foods USA (www.heritagefoodsusa .com) sells rare varieties of pork, beef, and poultry from animals that are on the brink of extinction. Because most commercial meats are raised from animals that are inbred and therefore genetically inferior, by purchasing heritage meats you are actually helping to preserve endangered livestock species. These animals are humanely raised, and their foraged diet is supplemented with traceable natural feed; no antibiotics are given, and no genetic modification has taken place. People who dine on heritage meats claim the flavor, taste, and quality is clearly noticeable with the first savory bite.

- **For the organic-only eater:** Now that it is easier than ever to find fresh organic fruits and vegetables at any supermarket, source artisanal and hard-to-find treats like scones, cookies, and cakes made entirely from organic ingredients. San Francisco's Miette Organic Pâtisserie creates delightful bakery confections all from high-quality organic ingredients. The company ships nationwide, and the adorable packaging adds to the experience of receiving one of Miette's organic treats. Order online at www.miettecakes.com.

- **When globe trotting:** When traveling abroad, take some time to visit local supermarkets, gourmet shops, and candy stores. Stock up on unusual finds that will travel well in your suitcase and have a long shelf life: jams and jellies, teas and coffee, spices, preserved fruits, dried herbs, flavored vinegars and oils, packaged cookies and and biscuits. Whenever a special occasion comes along, just fill a wicker basket full of treats from around the world and give a taste of the world to the gift recipient.

# FOR THE WINE CONNOISSEUR: MIMOSA KIT

This gift is so simple and so classy that it's hard to imagine anyone not cheering when receiving it.

I used a vintage champagne bucket from an antique store, but you can substitute it with a galvanized bucket from the home improvement store. Add a bottle of Champagne, a handful of organic oranges, and a wooden citrus reamer. Add your own twist. For example, instead of oranges, use pomegranates. Instead of a mimosa kit, make a Bloody Mary kit with a bottle of organic tomato juice, a piece of fresh horseradish, a lemon, small bottles of vodka, and a small bottle of Tabasco.

TIP: This is perhaps my most favorite gift to give during the holidays—a perfect gift to help ring in the new year, too!

93

# Sexually frustrated moths & Champagne? I'll toast to that.

Normally, when giving the gift of wine, I would suggest seeking out a good quality organic variety that uses pressed grapes grown without pesticides or insecticides. Unfortunately, I can't offer the same advice when it comes to Champagne; a visit to most local wine shops will usually come up empty-handed when seeking out a sparkling organic variety.

There is good news: some of the world's best-known and beloved Champagnes do incorporate ecologically friendly and sustainable methods in the production of their time-tested, sparkly beverages.

One of the world's largest luxury goods companies, LVMH Group, owns leading Champagne producers Moët & Chandon and Veuve Clicquot Ponsardin, two prestigious labels that have been making bubbly since the mid-eighteenth century.

In a genius marriage of using high-tech science to combat an old problem that has faced grape growers for centuries, LVMH scientists came up with a safe, eco-friendly, and highly effective method to combat an infestation of grape moths threatening the valuable Champagne grape crops.

The larvae of the grape moth cause considerable damage to vineyards. The moths spin a superfine webbing around the grapes that encourages mold and rotting, and the development of harmful fruit flies.

Instead of spraying the grapes with toxic insecticides, the LVMH scientists came up with a method to sexually confuse the moths. They placed capsules on the vines that saturated the air with the pheromones from the moth's female counterpart. As the male moths desperately flew around the vineyards attempting to mate with the females, they eventually died from exhaustion or sexual frustration. In 2003, over 63 percent of the Veuve Clicquot crops were saved by incorporating this ingenious method.

# FOR FRESH FLOWER LOVERS: PERSONALIZED FLOWER VASES

*Materials*

**Glass flower vases**

**Self-adhesive alphabet stickers**

**Chalk**

**Glass paint (recommended: Delta's PermEnamel Glass Paint)**

When I was a magazine editor, a day rarely went by when someone wouldn't receive fresh flowers with a congratulatory note attached. Once the flowers wilted, out went the flowers and yet another boring glass vase was added to the growing pile in the kitchen commissary. Over time, a considerable collection grew. If your place of work sounds similar to mine, rescue these vases and give this project a try. Fill the new vases with fresh, organic flowers and give it to someone you love; if that person gave you the vase to begin with, it's okay to regift. Trust me, he or she will never know.

Start by scrubbing the vase clean inside and out; use hot, soapy water and let it air dry thoroughly. Use alphabet stickers (from the office supply store) and stick them on the outside of the vase, spelling whatever word or phrase your heart desires. Generously rub chalk all over each sticker and carefully peel off the sticker to reveal the clean silhouette of the letter. Dab little drops of glass paint inside the chalk outline; the chalk will keep the paint from dripping. A little paint goes a long way, but if you do make a mistake, just rinse the vase under water and start again. Prop the vase upright in a box with crushed paper underneath and let it dry thoroughly. Once dry, wipe the chalk off with a damp towel.

Simply Green Giving

# FOR EVERYONE: MONEY RING

If you think giving cold, hard cash is, well, a cold idea, here's a fun way to warm it up. Fold a bill into a wearable ring and present it in a ring box.

Step One: Start with the back of the bill.

Step Two: Fold the white border on the top and the bottom of the bill as precisely as possible, bending the strip to the front of the bill.

Steps Three and Four: Fold the bill in half and then do it again. If you've done this correctly, you'll see the denomination perfectly in the right-hand corner.

Step Five: Fold the white border on the right side and make another fold on the left side of the denomination, so that you have a perfectly square number.

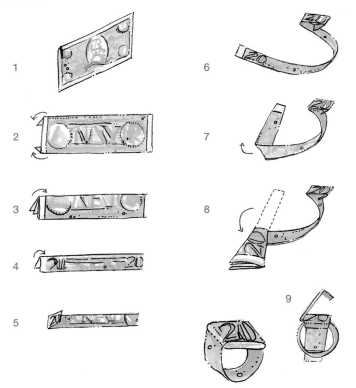

**Step Six:** Begin to curve the bill away from the folded square.

**Step Seven:** Make a 90-degree bend in the middle of the ring; be precise about this and use your finger to make a sharp crease.

**Step Eight:** Wrap the tail of the ring around, so it looks like a perfect L shape.

**Step Nine:** Loop the number part around the 90-degree bend section and continue wrapping the excess "tail" of the ring around until you've used it all up. Tuck it in and you've got yourself a ring.

## FOR THE SHOPAHOLIC: SHOPPING SPREE
## GIFT-CARD BAG

*Materials*

Four prepaid gift cards

Scotch tape

Hole punch

18-gauge wire

Beads

Gift cards are an ecological idea because you won't risk choosing an unwanted gift for someone. With a gift card, your friends can choose exactly what they need. If they are also ecologically minded, they can recycle the gift card by refilling it with money and giving the same card away as a present.

Handing someone a gift card, while much appreciated, doesn't have much charm or surprise to it. Give someone a "shopping spree" by making a handful of gift cards into a mini shopping bag.

Start with four gift cards; it's usually best to get four different cards from four different shops, hence the "spree" in the name of this project. But it's okay to use four cards from the same store.

Tape the cards together to form a box. Using the hole punch, punch two holes at the top of one card and two holes in another card directly across from the one you just punched. Attach an 18-gauge wire piece, roughly 4 inches in length, to one side. Thread beads—these are just inexpensive faux crystal ones from the craft store—until you have about ½ inch of wire at the end; wire the end to the other side. Repeat with the second set of holes.

TIP: When punching holes, be sure not to punch the gift card's magnetic strip. This might alter the effectiveness of the card.

103

# When a card is not just a card

I love paper cards over e-cards because they are more personal for and meaningful to the recipient. When sending a greeting or congratulatory note to someone, you don't just have to send a card. With a few additions and special touches, a card can become a keepsake the person will treasure for years. You can also slip a gift card inside these cards:

- **Make it glitter:** Highlight a portion on the front of the card with real glass glitter. Just brush white craft glue on a specific area (e.g., the large letters reading "Happy Birthday" or the wing on a bird illustration) and then sprinkle with glitter. Tap the card on a paper-covered surface to remove the excess and allow to dry completely; any white glue showing will dry clear.

- **Make it 3-D:** Glue buttons all over the card to fill in a tree or the backdrop. Snip small silk flowers off an old arrangement and glue them all over the inside. Cut out a photo of yourself and put yourself into the "scene" on the front of the card. Be creative and add things from the junk drawer to give the card depth and life.

- **A week of wishes:** To extend the thoughtfulness further, give a week's worth of cards. Pull out all those unused gift cards that you got from your favorite clothing store and write a different personal note on seven different cards. Seal them up in separate envelopes and tie them all together with a piece of ribbon. On the front of each card, write each day of the week, and instruct the recipient to open just one card per day.

- The "I'm sorry" card: Take a humiliating digital picture of yourself and slip it inside the card. If you goofed, at least now the recipient has ammo for the next time you screw things up!

- Give a recyclable card: For Valentine's Day, give your sweetie a recyclable card that instructs him or her to check off a box. Inside the card ask "Do you . . . love me, really love me, or really, really love me?" It's a sweet reminder of young love. Just don't get caught passing it in class!

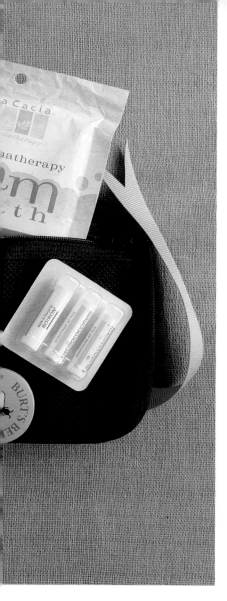

## FOR THE ROAD WARRIOR: SPA-TO-GO DOP KIT

This gift is a great to give to a road warrior or as a parting gift to someone who has traveled far to visit you: an inflight spa amenity gift.

Purchase the smallest dop kit you can find. This one is actually a tri-fold wallet with a carrying strap that goes around the neck.

Fill it with the smallest spa-type items you can find. This one contains several bags of antioxidant-rich green tea, Emergen-C vitamin powder, teeth-whitening and pore-unclogging strips, natural lip balm, small vials of homeo-pathic medicine to ward off colds, and an aromatherapy foaming bath packet that'll turn any hotel room into a relax-ing spa.

Make sure the finished kit is small enough to carry on the plane; if it's too bulky or heavy, you might add to the recipient's travel stress!

TIP: If making multiple kits, buy amenities in bulk and break them up to save on packaging and money.

## FOR THE NEW HOMEOWNER:
## WELCOME HOME GIFT

I love giving gifts that people can actually really use. I like it even better when it's totally eco-friendly.

Whenever a friend of mine moves into a new home, I send him or her a welcome home gift kit full of organic goodies that can be used right away.

To start, purchase a reusable, sturdy wood box from a home improvement or craft store. The box can be recycled to hold CDs or DVDs. Line it with

a folded nylon shower curtain; these shower curtains are far better for the planet because they do not need a liner, are not made from harmful vinyl, and can be easily cleaned in the washing machine. Next, add small necessities: a compact fluorescent light bulb (to save energy), an assortment of natural soaps, a scented soy candle, organic cotton hand towels, and your favorite all-natural beauty products.

WELCOME
HOME

# FOR THE DO-GOODER:
# A SAVE-THE-EARTH CHARM BRACELET

One of the fun things about poking around a junk shop is that you'll never know what you're going to uncover. In one of my favorite shops in Pennsylvania, I opened a dusty drawer simply marked "charming." Inside I found hundreds of vintage charms in all shapes and sizes, anything and everything the mind could imagine. The discovery gave me an idea.

Creating your own charm bracelet with real vintage pieces is much more personal and individual than those mass-produced, ready-to-wear ones at department stores. If you know someone who cares deeply about the world and does daily things to protect it, make a Save-the-Earth vintage charm bracelet.

Collect vintage charms that represent what the person is doing to give back to the earth. Link all the charms on a pretty bracelet and write a hand-written note explaining why you chose each charm. Here's a brief chart of some do-gooder charms I came up with, but feel free to add your own.

Cow: Vegetarian

Car or license plate: Drives a hybrid

Coin: Gives to charity

Shovel or Leaf: Grows an organic garden

Tree: Plants a tree

Sun: Uses solar energy

Cat or Dog: Adopts a stray animal

Peace sign: Has a peaceful soul

Clock or watch: Volunteers

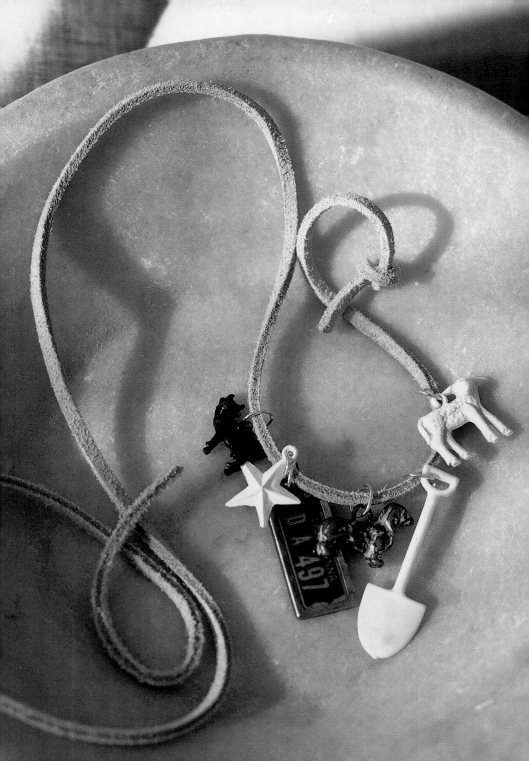

## FOR THE CANDLE LOVER: SWEET TREATS AND SWEET SCENTS

Soy candles aren't just better for the environment—they help perfume a room better. Since soy is clean-burning (meaning there's no smoke or soot emitted into the air when lit), the fragrance from the candle is cleaner and more noticeable when burning.

A nice present is a baker's dozen (or in this case, half dozen) sweetly scented soy candles along with fresh cupcakes from a local bakery. Pick up soy candles (I like www.itsasoy.com; their pumpkin pie and buttercream scented candles are amazing) and place them on a cookie sheet or tray. Surround them with cupcakes or other delectable treats such as cookies or even fresh doughnuts. What a great way to indulge!

# SIMPLY GREEN
## GIVING BACK

I can't imagine writing a book about the art of gift giving without sharing ways we can all give back to the world and make it a better place to live.

I began my career in activism around my twelfth birthday—the same day as Earth Day—when I was inspired to take action by all the gloom-and-doom stories of environmental devastation. Fortunately, because I was so young, I wasn't jaded or overwhelmed by the size of the problem. Instead, I was energized and excited to make a difference in the world. From those humble beginnings, I created a nonprofit organization and grew it into one of the country's largest teenage environmental activist groups.

Today, as one of the leaders in the eco-lifestyle field, I still think that giving back to the world is as important as giving an ecologically correct and stylish present. I believe it's an integral part of living a fulfilling, meaningful life. There is almost the same feeling of accomplishment when doing the seemingly small things, such as cleaning up a park or working on passing an eco-friendly law, like the healthy-schools legislation I worked on guaranteeing kids could learn in schools free of pesticides and insecticides. There are lessons even when you make the bigger changes, invaluable life lessons that shape your life and the world around us. Giving back can be one of the most selfish—but totally acceptable—things you do: you just *feel good* and learn so much from doing something altruistic. You become a stronger, smarter, better person.

People are always saying they would like to do something, but they don't have time. Activism, volunteerism, fund-raising, and just general acts of kindness don't have to be time-consuming or life-changing. You don't have to quit your job, give up all your worldly possessions, and fly off to a poverty-stricken Third World country to do good. It's all about multitasking and just making certain life decisions. It's about using what's available to you. It's about bringing friends and family along with you to help out.

## Getting Started

In New York City, in order to ride the subway system, you need to buy a plastic MetroCard to pass through the turnstile. At any given MetroCard vending machine, you'll see perfectly good cards strewn about all over the ground. This has been a big pet peeve of mine for one reason: These cards should be reusable, but for some reason the MTA (Metropolitan Transit Authority) didn't design their machines to accept used cards for most functions, and doesn't make any attempt to provide receptacles to collect them. This is just an obliviously messed-up situation that should be corrected. And with enough people voicing their opinion, it would be resolved. Fortunately, in the next few years the MTA will be moving away from the cards and toward more permanent and eco-friendly passes that are already in use in Europe and Japan.

Doing everyday small acts is really important when getting started because they are tiny exercises in improving your intuitive eco-senses. We all *know* what's wrong and right. But sometimes we don't realize how

wasteful we've become until it's pointed out to us. In the case of the MetroCards, anyone reading this who lives in or visits New York City will now have a hard time not noticing all those yellow cards littered all over the ground if they haven't already.

Try this: Think about every time you throw something away and how it got to this point in becoming trash. How many times have you gone to the ATM to withdraw cash and hit the "yes" button to get a printed receipt only to throw it immediately away? Why not press the "no" button and see your current balance on the screen instead? We usually press the "yes" button out of habit. It's time to break this wasteful habit.

How many times have you tossed a used coffee cup into an overflowing trash can, carefully placing your cup on top of an already teetering pile of trash? There's a very good chance that cup (along with others) will fall over and litter the streets. You see, the litter you find on the streets isn't put there by gross, trash-tossing, mean people—it's because the wind blows around whatever isn't securely discarded. The crazy,

crazy solution? Carry the empty cup to a different trash can that isn't full! Better yet, why not bring a reusable, stainless-steel cup with you to Starbucks and use it over and over again?

And think about this: When you use a public restroom, do you use a large sheet of paper towel to dry your hands? When you throw the towel away, do you notice the trash can overflowing with nothing but paper waste? Instead of hitting that lever six times to get a giant sheet of paper, hit it twice and use less. Sure, your hands might be a tiny bit wet when you're done, but at the end of the day, it's just water. They'll dry.

It's the little things that help you realize how impactful we all are on the Earth without even realizing it. Pay attention: Start turning off lights when you leave a room. Unplug electronics from the wall when you go away for vacation. Fix that dripping faucet in the bathroom and save some water. Your intuitive sense will begin to kick in real soon. You see, you can't really begin to care about the environment if your habitual actions aren't corrected. And here's the best part: Once you realize how wasteful your small actions can be, pretty soon you'll start to realize how we all waste money, too.

## Giving money

After I started my environmental group, I looked forward to future birthdays and holidays because it meant my parents would give me a gift of money. It was a very Korean thing to do; in lieu of gifts, Korean parents often give their children cash (neatly folded inside an envelope) as a present.

As strange as it sounds, I never actually bought anything with the money. Instead I would get cashier's checks, payable to various environmental groups, and send them as my membership dues or as additional contributions. These charitable donations were kept a secret from my parents—much like a teenager hiding cigarettes—because I knew they'd be upset to learn I had given away all the money. But once the nonprofit magazines and newsletters started to flood the mailbox, my secret was no more: My parents set a rule that I had to splurge on myself.

Looking back, I now understand why my parents didn't want me to selflessly give everything away; after all, a twelve-year-old shouldn't be responsible for the world's problems—let the adults handle it. In retrospect, it makes my argument with my mother in the supermarket over phosphate-free detergents much more humorous.

But now, as an adult, I feel it's important to continue to give cold, hard cash to charities. Nonprofit groups need cash to both purchase land for the prevention of it being destroyed by development and fund scientific studies to combat global warming. They need money to pay the bills so lobbyists working to push *good* laws can work in a nice, efficient office. Sure, many of us think we're doing a heroic act by donating our old computer to charity, but think about this: If the computer didn't work for *you*, why would it work for *them*?

My rule of thumb for giving is twofold: Give cash to charities you wholeheartedly support and know will do a good job with your donation, and raise money in the most efficient and successful way possible.

Figure out whatever cause you truly, absolutely believe in. Do your research and determine who is spending wisely, who is effective, and who can use the money now. Donate as if you're investing in the stock market—while a five-hundred-dollar contribution to a struggling charity will generate gushing thank-you notes, their financial woes may mean your check is used to pay debt, not to save the world. On the other hand, giving to an established charity may not get you a handwritten note, but it'll add to an important coffer that collectively *could*

actually change the world! But then again, that five hundred dollars could be so useful to a community group that wants to restore a local park. Again, it's all about doing your homework of *how* the money will be used.

Raising money doesn't have to mean bake sales and car washes. In fact, it's not about fund-raising at all. When I purchased my 1921 bungalow in Pennsylvania, the purchase came with one stipulation: all the furniture (love it or hate it) was included in the sale. The furniture was antique pieces, but definitely not my style. So I arranged for a local auction house to come and take it away and sell it off the following weekend. Since the furniture sale was quite literally found money, I treated myself to a new furniture purchase from the proceeds and donated the remaining half to charity. I get a nice tax deduction and my bank account balance stays the same.

Look in your own life for situations where found money for you can be real money for charity. Got a huge jar of pennies on the kitchen counter? Bring it to change-counting machine and either elect to give it all to charity right away, or write a check in the amount of the spare change. Shopping for a major purchase online? Buy through an affinity Web site that donates up to 10 percent of the purchase price to the charity of your choice; that can really add up, and you did nothing more than just click on the right Web page. Replacing your computer or old cell phone? You may be able to sell them to an online electronic parts buyer. Again, it was trash to you, so why not write a check to your favorite charity in the amount you receive?

In most situations, many of us would just toss the computer out into the trash. But with a little research, you can be less wasteful and recycle it *and* raise money for charity. My motto is really simple: Waste not, because someone else may want it.

## Inspiring Kids

When I started my environmental crusade, I had a call to action from reading the morning newspaper. I was altogether scared, inspired, and empowered to take charge. A call to action is exactly what it sounds like: something happens in the world, your community, or your personal life that makes you realize that you've got to do something—anything—to turn what's wrong into right. While most kids won't run off and start a nonprofit group from watching the evening news, there are things you can do to make them more aware that the world doesn't revolve around them.

Encouraging tomorrow's leaders to care about the environment is an easier cause than many others. First, young people are generally drawn to the green cause since it's the entire world around them: trees, animals, the sky, the oceans. It's pretty straightforward: Who wouldn't want to see gorgeous trees, innocent animals and blue skies be saved?

- With toddlers, you can start by feeding them a diet rich in organic foods, ultimately produced locally. Today, it's easier than ever to find affordable organic food at most supermarkets. Remember generic food from the distant past? It was in the black-and-white, no-frills packaging emblazoned with straightforward words like CORN or PEACHES. Today, no-frills has been replaced by store brands, which are beautifully packaged and high-quality. Many store brands offer organic staples—milk, eggs, cereal, frozen vegetables—that are free of harmful pesticides and insecticides and also inexpensive because they are manufactured direct-to-consumer. Sure, he's not going to notice the mushy peas are organic, but it's a nice way to bring your tyke up in the world.

- You can also show young children that recycling can be fun. What child doesn't like to draw with crayons? But, if they're like my nephew, they prefer to draw with fresh, sharp crayons, not the worn-down remnants usually tossed out. You can recycle crayons with your kids very easily. Just sort them by color (they can help you with that) and peel off the paper labels. Fill microwaveable Pyrex measuring cups with crayons—reds, blues, greens—and melt them in the microwave. Pour the melted wax into plastic candy molds available at any craft store (keep small hands away—it's hot) and let them chill up in the fridge. Pop them out and voilà! New crayons! The molds come in many different shapes and sizes; what kid wouldn't love to draw with crayons in the shape of worms, flowers, or seashells?

- As children get older, consider buying them a membership in an environmental or animal protection organization. Many organizations have youth divisions that create educational materials (e.g., newsletters and magazines) specifically written for kids. You can get them a subscription as a present or stocking stuffer and the monthly or quarterly publication will be real mail, addressed just to them!

Finally and most importantly, let your kids see *you* in action—so that giving back becomes the norm, not the exception. When you're shopping at the supermarket, make it a habit to pick up a few essentials each week that you donate to charity. Ask them to pick a nonprofit group to whom you'll send a check each month. Visit the home improvement store and have each child pick out a tree; plant it in the yard and let them watch it grow as they grow older, too. Twice a year, ask them to pick toys and clothes they no longer want and bring them together to Goodwill or the Salvation Army store for donation; explain why you're donating.

Whether it's being more aware of things you throw away, giving money to charity, or guiding a child onto a path of altruistic enlightenment, there is no excuse not to do something—anything—every day. Look beyond these ideas and come up with your own. Read the newspaper and see what's impacting your community, and if there's anything you can do to help. It really can be simple.

# Giving gifts of charity

A popular form of gift giving is to not actually purchase a present for someone, but to give money to charity in the recipient's name. While you're being altruistic and getting that warm, fuzzy feeling for helping to make a difference, you can't help but wonder if the recipient's "Oh, how sweet," comment is genuine or a cover for disappointment in not receiving a real gift.

You can, however, give to charity and make everyone happy with these simple ideas when giving to some popular charities:

- Habitat for Humanity (www.habitat.org): Since 1976, Habitat for Humanity has built over 175,000 homes in over 100 countries to help provide people with decent, affordable shelter. Habitat builds so many homes each year that it claims to build a new home every 26 minutes for a family in need. When giving a donation to Habitat for Humanity in someone's name, give the recipient a *Simply Green* doormat made out of recycled rubber, natural sisal, or sturdy metal grate (will last forever) along with a note explaining the donation is helping someone else get a home, too.

- The Humane Society of the United States (HSUS) (www.hsus.org): HSUS, founded in 1954, is the largest animal protection organization in the United States. Today it has nearly 10 million members working together to help all types of animals. You can sign someone up as a member for just twenty-five dollars and that person will receive a subscription to the organization's award-winning *All Animals* magazine. Tie a gift card outlining the donation to a brand-new bird feeder to show your gift is helping animals.

- UNICEF (www.unicef.org): The United Nations Children's Fund is a broad international coalition dedicated to improving the life of every child around the globe. With a presence in over 157 countries, UNICEF projects run the gamut of preventing the spread of HIV/AIDS among young people, giving young girls a proper education, and immunizing young children against diseases. Giving a monetary gift to UNICEF is a wonderful gift to give in someone's name, especially if he or she recently had a child; give a small baby item—such as a recycled cashmere baby beanie—along with your gift card donation to UNICEF to complete the gift.

- Natural Resources Defense Council (NRDC) (www.nrdc .org): NRDC is an environmental, political, and scientific powerhouse that is a polluter's or corrupt politician's worst enemy. NRDC's mission is broad but simple: "to safeguard the Earth: its people, its plants and animals and the natural systems on which all life depends." Through litigation, political action, and grassroots campaigns, NRDC has achieved many groundbreaking successes that are ensuring a brighter, cleaner future for all. Sign up a friend with an NRDC membership and include a set of energy-saving solar outdoor lights; when the lights brighten up the nighttime sky, the recipient will continuously be reminded of your eco-friendly gift.

# RESOURCES

Almost all of the projects in this book can be made with everyday materials from around the house. If you're missing a supply or two, the following resources are good places to locate the hard-to-find items I used in this book. It's always best to patronize local shops whenever possible, but when you can't, online shopping can't be beat.

## Bamboo Steamers

Every city seems to have an Asian market now, so look there first because there will be a big selection to choose from and you'll save on shipping.

Cooking.com, www.cooking.com; Williams-Sonoma, www.williams-sonoma.com

## Bandannas

Local Army & Navy stores will have the best selection.

Galaxy Army & Navy, www.galaxayarmynavy.com

## Cellophane Rolls

Try your local restaurant supply store first to see if it sells large rolls of cellophane; it's always useful to have on hand, and you'll save money when you buy in bulk.

MisterArt, www.misterart.com

## Champagne

For more information on LVMH's sustainability practices with their brands Veuve Clicquot Ponsardin and Moët & Chandon, visit www.lvmh.com. For ideas on recycling Champagne corks into a charming trivet, check out my previous book, *Simply Green Parties*.

## Cigar Boxes

Your best bet is to visit a local cigar shop and pick them out yourself. eBay is not a good choice to buy inexpensive cigar boxes; I've only found antique and vintage varieties that hardcore collectors will pay a premium for. The online site Cigar.com (www.cigar.com) does sell single manufacturer boxes, which range from the elaborate to the simple, but it chooses the box for you.

## Contact Paper

I always find rolls of this stuff at Goodwill. You can also try discount retailers, such as Kmart.

Kmart, www.kmart.com

## Electrical Tape

You'll find rolls of this tape in the lighting section of most home improvement stores.

The Home Depot, www.homedepot.com; Lowe's, www.lowes .com

## Glass Paint

Delta's PermEnamel Glass Paint, www.deltacrafts.com

## Glycerin Soap and Soap Making Supplies

Michaels, www.michaels.com

## Hemp String and Twine

I use hemp string all the time because of its durability. Hemp is $1\frac{1}{2}$ times stronger than most twine and string. Hemp Traders, www.hemptraders.com

## Hole Punches

Even though the cheaper varieties may seem like a bargain, they aren't; they break and won't punch through thicker papers. I prefer Fiskars brand punches, which really do work well and are worth the extra money. Fiskars, www.fiskars.com

## Ink Pads & Alphabet Stamp Kits

A.C. Moore, www.acmoore.com; Kate's Paperie, www.katespaperie.com; Michaels, www.michaels.com

## Stitch Witchery Fabric-Binding Tape

One roll of this tape will really go a long way. Hancock Fabrics, www.hancockfabrics.com

Resources

## Terra-Cotta Pots and Gardening Supplies

Terra-cotta pots are easy to break, so it's best to purchase them at local home improvement stores. If you do order them from a catalog, keep in mind they are going to be packed in layers of protective packaging, which is never good for the environment. For more exotic finishes and shapes, I like Gardener's Supply Company (www.gardeners.com) and Smith & Hawken (www.smithandhawken.com)

## Vintage Charms

It's always best to choose charms in person, so you can get a feel for the size, finish, and quality (and bargain the price down, too). Be on the lookout for flea markets, yard sales, and antique stores all year-round. You can also try online sellers like eBay (www.ebay.com) for that one hard-to-find charm.

## Wood Boxes

I prefer the very thin, wood-veneer boxes made by a company called Nicole. They look more elegant, are not as bulky as most wood boxes, and are inexpensive.

A.C. Moore, www.acmoore.com

# Index

Danny Seo is America's environmental lifestyle expert on stylish, eco-friendly living. He is the author of four books, including *Simply Green Parties*, (Collins, 2006). Danny is the host, creator, and executive producer of the TV series *Simply Green with Danny Seo* on LIME: Healthy Living with a Twist, and host of the companion program of the same name on SIRIUS Satellite Radio. He is a contributing editor to *Country Home* magazine, and his work on eco-friendly style has appeared in *USA Today, People, Elle, Food & Wine, Parade*, and on *The Oprah Winfrey Show, The View*, and *Today*. Danny is the spokesperson for "Call2Recycle," a nationwide, nonprofit cell phone and rechargeable battery recycling campaign. He is also the official eco-stylist for Kimpton Hotel & Restaurant Group, a collection of upscale boutique properties nationwide. Danny proudly supports the Humane Society of the United States. Learn more at www .dannyseo.com.

Jennifer Levy is a New York–based photographer specializing in lifestyle, design, and food. Her work appears in numerous magazines including *Metropolitan Home, Martha Stewart Living*, and *Better Homes and Gardens*. She has photographed more than fourteen books and was both photographer and author of *Kids' Rooms: Ideas and Projects for Children's Spaces* (Chronicle, 2001). In addition to photography assignments, her current project is the design and renovation of a Brooklyn townhouse, which—should she survive—will house herself, her partner (filmmaker Art Jones), and her son, Edison.

# Look for Danny Seo's new DVD from *lime* :

## simple steps to a greener home

Available as a part of LIME's *Simple Steps* series.
To order, please visit **lime.com/danny**

Choices we make every day have an impact on our planet. Inside this DVD you will find projects, ideas, and simple tips that prove that style and sustainability can go hand in hand and even save you money.

Come into my home and see how I've transformed it into a chic, green living space.

It's easy to do and I'll show you how!

— Danny Seo

Includes:

- Product recommendations for every room in your home, from flooring to bedding to walls

- A guide to energy-saving appliances and lighting

- The truth about composting

- Saving money on heating and cooling

- Cleaning your home the nontoxic way

139

For more on Danny Seo and other ways to live a healthier, greener, more balanced life, visit **lime.com/danny**

# ALSO FROM DANNY SEO

## Simply Green
### *Parties*

*Simple and Resourceful Ideas for Throwing the Perfect Celebration, Event, or Get-together*

ISBN 0-06-112271-8

Danny Seo, the eco-conscious and creative wonder kid, presents simple and gorgeous ideas for throwing the perfect party.

### Dining Under the Stars
Paint glow-in-the-dark rocks to lead guests to a magical dining spot

### A Twist on a Birthday Party
Make a spa piñata and candles that reveal treasures as they burn

### A Spring Baby Shower
Five-minute, handmade stylish invites and fresh organic food ideas

### Sizzling Summer Party
Turn shopping bags into flower vases in three easy steps

### Your Housewarming Party
Create instant heirloom home décor with leftover construction materials

### Winter Warm Up
Stay cozy with your friends with reupholstered sweater chairs